Hey Diddle Diddle

Hey Diddle Diddle

By Leonard Kessler

GARRARD PUBLISHING COMPANY
CHAMPAIGN, ILLINOIS

To Jackie Meyer

Library of Congress Cataloging in Publication Data

Kessler, Leonard P
    Hey diddle diddle.

    (Young Mother Goose books)
    SUMMARY: A traditional nursery rhyme is expanded to
include a tuba-playing cat, a singing rug, a flying
whale, and a horse who eats pickles.
    1. Children's poetry, American. [1. Nursery
rhymes. 2. American poetry] I. Title.
II. Series.
PS3561.E675H4   398.8   79-18966
ISBN 0-8116-7403-9

Hey Diddle Diddle

Hey diddle diddle,

The cat and the fiddle,

The cow jumped over the moon.

The little dog laughed

To see such sport,

And the dish ran away with the spoon.

Hey diddle doodles,

The goat ate some noodles.

The elephant sat in the sink.

The monkey did tricks
All through the night,
And the purple cows all became pink.

9

Hey diddle rickle,

The horse ate a pickle.

The donkey fell through the ice.

The ox and fox
Wore new purple socks,
And the hippo ate meatballs with rice.

Hey diddle dandy,

The crab ate the candy.

The whale flew high in the air.

The yellow fish laughed,
"You funny whale,"
And the crab said, "I really don't care!"

Hey diddle diddle,

The cat and the fiddle,

The horse flew up in the tree.

The little frog laughed
To see the sight,
And the fly kissed the big bumblebee.

Hey diddle dumpkin,
A witch grabbed her pumpkin.
The cookies jumped over the fence.

The kangaroo slid
Down from the house,
And the dime ran off with five cents.

Hey diddle dunkle,

The ant called her uncle

On the shiny old telephone.

The crow threw a pie,

Hit fly in the eye.

And the duck said, "Please let him alone!"

Hey diddle diddle,
The frog heard a riddle.
The hog flew in a balloon.

The ants on the plants
Jitterbug danced,
And the rug sang a jolly good tune.

Hey diddle daddle,

The cat had the paddle.

The owl sat on the big log.

The little dog laughed,
"That's not a boat,"
And the elephant danced with the frog.

Hey diddle dibble,

The mouse took a nibble.

"Give me some more, won't you please?"

The little cat laughed,
"You silly mouse,
Why do you eat onions with cheese?"

Hey diddle dooba,

The cat played the tuba.

The cow got stuck in the door.

The little pig laughed
To see such sights,
And the door danced around on the floor.

Hey diddle dilly,
The duck is so silly.
She bit the old kangaroo.

And the big brown bear
Danced with the chair,
And they all sang
"Skip-Skip-to-My-Lou."

29

So it's . . .

Hey diddle diddle,

The cat and the fiddle,

The cow jumped up to the moon.

The men on the moon

Were very surprised

When the cow flew away on a spoon!

LEGO® CITY

ADVENTURES

HELP IS ON THE WAY!

By Sonia Sander

By Sonia Sander
Illustrated by Mada Design

SCHOLASTIC INC.

NEW YORK   TORONTO   LONDON   AUCKLAND

SYDNEY   MEXICO CITY   NEW DELHI   HONG KONG

But he hasn't.
No one Jessie asks has seen Bear.
Oh, no, poor Bear is lost.

14

Jessie hears Bear cry.
She finds him in the park.
Poor Bear is stuck under a gate!

Bear needs help fast.
Jessie asks the police for help.

24

C-r-r-r-e-e-a-a-k-k!
Jessie's new friends lift
the gate off Bear.

27

The workers take good care of Bear.
They wrap up his paw.

29

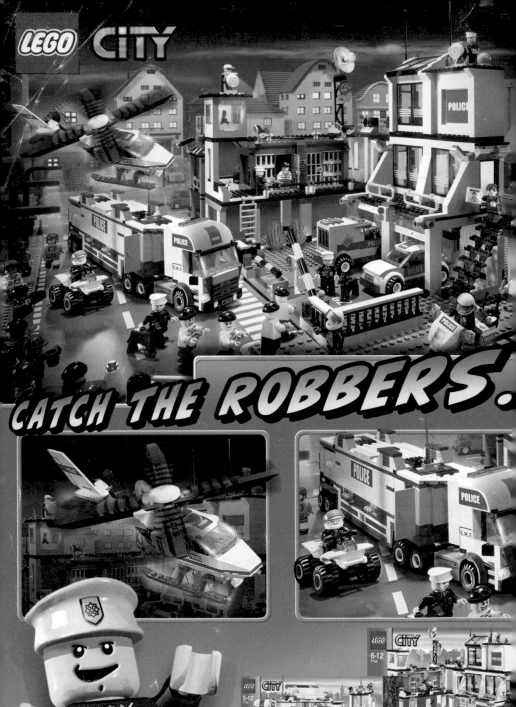

LEGO CITY

CATCH THE ROBBERS.

...WITH THE LEGO® CITY POLICE COLLEC

- Catch the robbers with the police truck
- Take them to the police station
- Lock them up in the prison block